BAKE YOUR OWN
BROWNIES

BY MARI BOLTE

PEBBLE
a capstone imprint

Published by Pebble, an imprint of Capstone
1710 Roe Crest Drive, North Mankato, Minnesota 56003
capstonepub.com

Copyright © 2026 by Capstone. All rights reserved. No part of this publication may be reproduced in whole or in part, or stored in a retrieval system, or transmitted in any form or by any means, electronic, mechanical, photocopying, recording, or otherwise, without written permission of the publisher.

Library of Congress Cataloging-in-Publication Data
Names: Bolte, Mari, author.
Title: Bake your own brownies / by Mari Bolte.
Description: North Mankato, Minnesota : Pebble, an imprint of Capstone, [2026] | Series: Pebble maker baking | Audience: Ages 5–8 | Audience: Grades 2–3 | Summary: "Craving chocolate goodness? Early and emergent readers can bake their own batch of yummy, fudgy brownies! Step-by-step instructions plus clear photos guide elementary children through this simple and sweet recipe that they (with a little adult assistance) can make themselves—and then enjoy!"— Provided by publisher.
Identifiers: LCCN 2024048980 (print) | LCCN 2024048981 (ebook) | ISBN 9798875224225 (hardcover) | ISBN 9798875224171 (paperback) | ISBN 9798875224188 (pdf) | ISBN 9798875224195 (epub) | ISBN 9798875224201 (kindle edition)
Subjects: LCSH: Brownies (Cooking)—Juvenile literature. | LCGFT: Cookbooks.
Classification: LCC TX771 .B65 2026 (print) | LCC TX771 (ebook) | DDC 641.86/53—dc23/eng/20241205
LC record available at https://lccn.loc.gov/2024048980
LC ebook record available at https://lccn.loc.gov/2024048981

Editorial Credits
Editor: Abby Cich; Designer: Heidi Thompson; Media Researcher: Jo Miller; Production Specialist: Tori Abraham

Image Credits
Capstone: Karon Dubke, front and back cover, 1, 9, 10, 12–17, 19, 21; Shutterstock: Amaliya_Barsegova, 5, conzorb, 11, nadianb, 23, PeopleImages.com - Yuri A, 7

The publisher and the author shall not be liable for any damages allegedly arising from the information in this book, and they specifically disclaim any liability from the use or application of any of the contents of this book.

Any additional websites and resources referenced in this book are not maintained, authorized, or sponsored by Capstone. All product and company names are trademarks™ or registered® trademarks of their respective holders.

Printed and bound in China. 6274

TABLE OF CONTENTS

Sweet Mistake 4

Kitchen Tips 6

What You Need 8

What You Do 10

Take It Further 22

Glossary 24

About the Author 24

Words in **BOLD** are in the glossary.

SWEET MISTAKE

Brownies have been enjoyed for more than 100 years. One story says they were first made by mistake! A baker was making chocolate cake. They forgot baking powder. The cake did not rise. But it still tasted good.

Bake your own tasty brownies, on purpose!

KITCHEN TIPS

Stay safe and have fun with these tips.

- Have an adult helper nearby. Ask them to help with hot or sharp things.

- Read the recipe before you start. Get all your **ingredients** and tools.

- Wash your hands before you begin.

- Help clean up when you are done!

WHAT YOU NEED

INGREDIENTS

- 3/4 cup (170 grams) salted butter
- 1 cup (213 g) brown sugar
- 1 cup (198 g) white sugar
- 3 eggs
- 1 tablespoon (15 milliliters) vanilla **extract**
- 1 cup (120 g) flour
- 3/4 cup (63 g) **cocoa powder**
- 1/2 teaspoon (3 g) salt

TOOLS

- 8-inch (20.3-centimeter) square baking pan
- **cooking spray**
- measuring cups and spoons
- large microwave-safe bowl
- mixing spoon
- small bowl
- fork
- cooling rack

WHAT YOU DO

STEP 1

Spray the inside of the baking pan with cooking spray. Ask an adult to **preheat** the oven to 350°F (175°C).

STEP 2

Put the butter in the large bowl. With the adult's help, heat the butter in the microwave. Go 30 seconds at a time until it is melted.

Stir in the brown and white sugars until smooth.

STEP 3

Crack the eggs into the small bowl. Take out any shell pieces. Give the eggs a good stir with the fork to break them up.

Pour the eggs into the large bowl. Add the vanilla extract. Stir it all together.

STEP 4

Add the flour, cocoa powder, and salt to the large bowl. Stir gently. Go till the **batter** is all dark brown.

Pour the batter into the pan.

STEP 5

Ask the adult to put the brownies in the oven. Bake them for 35 to 45 minutes. The middle should look **set**. To check, ask the adult to gently shake the pan. Is there no jiggle? That means the brownies are done!

STEP 6

Let the brownies cool for 30 to 60 minutes. Then, ask an adult to cut them into 16 pieces.

Enjoy! Keep extras in a dish with a lid.

TAKE IT FURTHER

Add 1/4 cup (43 g) chocolate chips on top of your brownies before baking. You can also try mint or peanut butter chips.

Use another extract. Almond, coconut, or orange is tasty! Use 1/2 teaspoon (2.5 mL).

Make your brownies into fun shapes! Use cookie cutters to cut pieces from the pan.

GLOSSARY

batter (BAT-uhr)—a wet mixture that can be poured, usually made of at least flour and a liquid

cocoa powder (KOH-koh POW-duhr)—a dry, brown powder that is made from cacao beans and has a rich, chocolate-y taste

cooking spray (KOOK-ing SPRAY)—an oil that is sprayed onto cookware and bakeware to keep food from sticking

extract (EK-strakt)—a liquid used for flavoring food

ingredient (in-GREE-dee-uhnt)—a food that is put with other foods to make a recipe

preheat (PREE-heet)—to heat an oven to a certain temperature before baking

set (SEHT)—firm; in baking, "set" means the middle of a baked good no longer looks liquid-y

ABOUT THE AUTHOR

Mari Bolte has been baking—and writing books about baking—since the beginning of time. (Well, it feels like that, anyway.) These days, she squeezes in loaves of no-knead bread and trays of sweet treats in between writing projects.